Our Family Tree

Mike Jackson

Illustrated by

Diana Bowles

Evans

Be careful with them. Some of the
photos in there are very old.

That's your Great-great-great grandpa
Samuel. That picture was taken about a
hundred years ago.

He is fixing a shoe to a horse's hoof. He
was a blacksmith, just like his father.
Samuel was married to Agatha, so she is
your Great-great-great grandma.

They are your Great-great grandma Maud, and her two sisters, Ethel and Martha.

Martha married an American soldier during the first world war and went to live in America. They went in a big ocean liner. I think her husband became a farmer.

Ethel died when she was only 18. People often died young in those days because there was no proper medicine.

Let's take the albums downstairs
and I'll draw you a family tree.

It's a diagram that shows where everybody fits into a family. It has dates so that you know when somebody was born and when they died.

Here is the first part of our family tree.

Great-great-great
grandpa Samuel
(1865-1950)

Great-great-great
grandma Agatha
(1870-1958)

Theodore
(1890-1957)

Wilfred
(1891-1917)

Ethel
(1892-1910)

Great-great
grandma
Maud
(1893-1968)

Martha
(1894-1962)

Kathleen
(1896-1970)

Harriet
(1902-1968)

Your Great-great grandma Maud had two other brothers and two other sisters. Their names were Theodore, Wilfred, Kathleen and Harriet.

So altogether there were seven children.

That's a big family!

People often had big families in those days.

Maud married Stanley and they had three children — Winifred, Arthur and Edith. Winifred was your Great grandma.

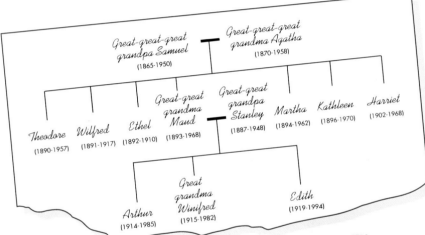

Great-great-great grandpa Samuel (1865-1950) — Great-great-great grandma Agatha (1870-1958)

Theodore (1890-1957)   Wilfred (1891-1917)   Ethel (1892-1910)   Great-great grandma Maud (1893-1968) — Great-great grandpa Stanley (1887-1948)   Martha (1894-1962)   Kathleen (1896-1970)   Harriet (1902-1968)

Arthur (1914-1985)   Great grandma Winifred (1915-1982)   Edith (1919-1994)

Let's see if I can find their photographs.

Is this one, Grandma?

Yes, that is your Great grandma Winifred. She was my Mother.

Look at the funny old car.

17

And here is your Great grandpa, my Father. His name was Frank.

What did he do?

18

He was a train driver. In those days trains were powered by steam. Here's another picture of him in his cab.

Who do you think this baby is?

It must be you, Grandma!

What a funny pram!

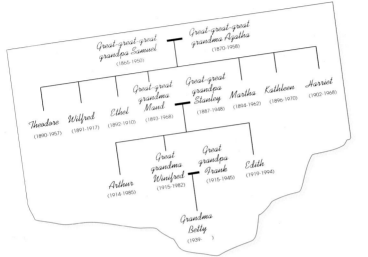

Great-great-great
grandpa Samuel
(1865-1950)

Great-great-great
grandma Agatha
(1870-1958)

Theodore
(1890-1957)

Wilfred
(1891-1917)

Ethel
(1892-1910)

Great-great
grandma
Maud
(1893-1968)

Great-great
grandpa
Stanley
(1887-1948)

Martha
(1894-1962)

Kathleen
(1896-1970)

Harriet
(1902-1968)

Arthur
(1914-1985)

Great
grandma
Winifred
(1915-1982)

Great
grandpa
Frank
(1915-1945)

Edith
(1919-1994)

Grandma
Betty
(1939-   )

21

No, that's my brother Tom saying
goodbye to my Father.

My Father joined the army and died
fighting in the second world war.

Here's a picture of your Grandpa Sidney and me on our wedding day. That was over thirty years ago.

He was a shipbuilder. There aren't many shipbuilders left in this country today.

I'll bet you can't guess
who this is.

And that must be Uncle Paul.

We often took holidays by the sea when your Mother was a child.

Now our family tree is nearly finished,
but who's missing?

Great-great-great
grandpa Samuel
(1865-1950) — Great-great-great
grandma Agatha
(1870-1958)

Theodore (1890-1957) Wilfred (1891-1917) Ethel (1892-1910) Great-great grandma Maud (1893-1968) Great-great grandpa Stanley (1887-1948) Martha (1894-1962) Kathleen (1896-1970) Harriet (1902-1968)

Arthur (1914-1985) Great grandma Winifred (1915-1982) — Great grandpa Frank (1915-1945) Edith (1919-1994)

Tom (1941-) Grandma Betty (1939-) — Grandpa Sidney (1938-)

Mum (1965-) — Dad (1962-) Uncle Paul (1967-)

Us, of course!

That's right. We'll put your names at the
bottom — Tom, Kelly and Tammy.

> But we could draw another family tree, couldn't we, Grandma?

Yes, you could draw a family tree of your
Father's side of the family. I expect
Grandpa Peter has lots of old pictures
you could look at, too.

Here is Tom, Kelly and Tammy's family tree with some of the words missing. Can you remember who the people are? The answers are below, but don't peep until you have tried yourself.

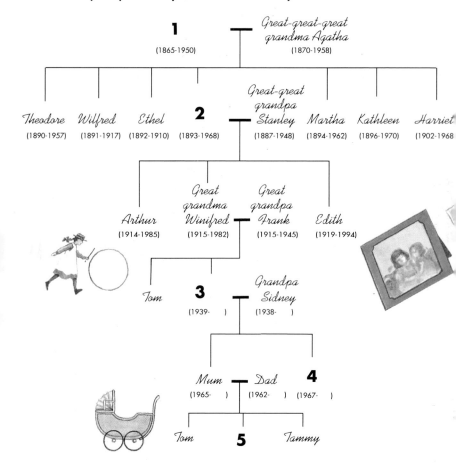

1
(1865-1950)

Great-great-great grandma Agatha
(1870-1958)

Theodore
(1890-1957)

Wilfred
(1891-1917)

Ethel
(1892-1910)

2
(1893-1968)

Great-great grandpa Stanley
(1887-1948)

Martha
(1894-1962)

Kathleen
(1896-1970)

Harriet
(1902-1968)

Arthur
(1914-1985)

Great grandma Winifred
(1915-1982)

Great grandpa Frank
(1915-1945)

Edith
(1919-1994)

Tom

3
(1939-   )

Grandpa Sidney
(1938-   )

Mum
(1965-   )

Dad
(1962-   )

4
(1967-   )

Tom

5

Tammy

3. Grandma Betty 4. Uncle Paul 5. Kelly

1. Great-great-great grandpa Samuel 2. Great-great Grandma Maud

30